A BOOK
ABOUT JESUS

AMERICAN BIBLE SOCIETY
NEW YORK

This Portion of Holy Scripture in the *Contemporary English Version* is part of the New Testament of our Lord Jesus Christ. The translation was made directly from the Greek text published by the Bible Societies and is not based on any other English translation.

For a free catalog of Scripture publications, call the American Bible Society at 1-800-32-BIBLE, or write to, 1865 Broadway, New York, N.Y. 10023.

Imprimatur
✠ Most Rev. Daniel E. Pilarczyk
President, National Conference of Catholic Bishops

Illustrated by Jane Dyer.

ISBN 1 – 58516 – 163 – 2

Printed in the United States of America
Eng. Port. CEV560P – 100871
ABS – 12/02 – 5,000 – 44,000 —RRD15

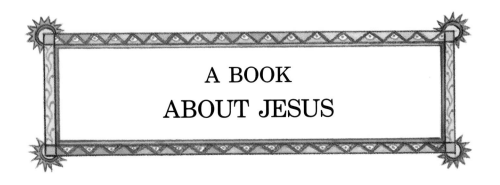

A BOOK
ABOUT JESUS

A Book About Jesus is a new and exciting translation of stories from the New Testament. It is written in language that young readers, as well as their parents and older friends, will understand and appreciate.

These stories tell about the birth of Jesus, some of the things he did and taught, and a few of the many people he helped. But most important is the story of how he died and then came back alive with all power in heaven and on earth.

Words which may be hard to understand are explained in the list of *Important Words to Know* at the back of the book. Unusual phrases and other difficult things are marked by a star (*) and are explained in *Notes* in the back of the book, where they are listed by page numbers.

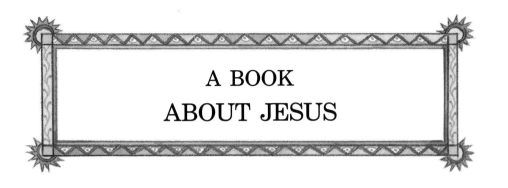

A BOOK
ABOUT JESUS

THE BEGINNING

The Birth of Jesus
(Matthew 1.18-23; Luke 2.1-7)

This is how Jesus Christ was born. A young woman named Mary was engaged to Joseph from King David's family. But before they were married, she learned that she was going to have a baby by God's Holy Spirit. Joseph was a good man* and did not want to embarrass Mary in front of everyone. So he decided to quietly call off the wedding.

While Joseph was thinking about this, an angel from the Lord came to him in a dream. The angel said, "Joseph, the baby that Mary will have is from the Holy Spirit. Go ahead and marry her. Then after her baby is born, name him Jesus,* because he will save his people from their sins."

So God's promise came true, just as the prophet had said, "A virgin will have a baby boy, and he will be called Immanuel," which means "God is with us."

About that time Emperor Augustus gave orders for the names of all the people to be listed in record books.* These first records were made when Quirinius was governor of Syria.*

Everyone had to go to their own hometown to be listed. So Joseph had to leave Nazareth in Galilee and go to Bethlehem in Judea. Long ago Bethlehem had been King David's hometown, and Joseph went there because he was from David's family.

Mary was engaged to Joseph and traveled with him to Bethlehem. She was soon going to have a baby, and while they were there, she gave birth to her first-born* son. She dressed him

9

in baby clothes* and laid him in a feed box, because there was no room for them in the inn.

The Shepherds
(Luke 2.8-20)

That night in the fields near Bethlehem some shepherds were guarding their sheep. All at once an angel came down to them from the Lord, and the brightness of the Lord's glory flashed around them. The shepherds were frightened. But the angel said, "Don't be afraid! I have good news for you, which will make everyone happy. This very day in King David's hometown a Savior was born for you. He is Christ the Lord. You will know who he is, because you will find him dressed in baby clothes and lying in a feed box."

Suddenly many other angels came down from heaven and joined in praising God. They said:

"Praise God in heaven!

Peace on earth to everyone

who pleases God."

After the angels had left and gone back to heaven, the shepherds said to each other, "Let's go to Bethlehem and see what the Lord has told us about." They hurried off and found Mary and Joseph, and they saw the baby lying in the feed box.

When the shepherds saw Jesus, they told his parents what the angel had said about him. Everyone listened and was surprised. But Mary kept thinking about all this and wondering what it meant.

As the shepherds returned to their sheep, they were

praising God and saying wonderful things about him. Everything they had seen and heard was just as the angel had said.

Simeon Praises the Lord
(Luke 2.22-32)

The time came for Mary and Joseph to do what the Law of Moses says a mother is supposed to do after her baby is born.*

They took Jesus to the temple in Jerusalem and presented him to the Lord, just as the Law of the Lord says, "Each first-born* baby boy belongs to the Lord." The Law of the Lord also says that parents have to offer a sacrifice, giving at least a pair of doves or two young pigeons. So that is what Mary and Joseph did.

At this time a man named Simeon was living in Jerusalem. Simeon was a good man. He loved God and was waiting for God to save the people of Israel. God's Spirit came to him and told him that he would not die until he had seen Christ the Lord.

When Mary and Joseph brought Jesus to the temple to do what the Law of Moses says should be done for a new baby, the Spirit told Simeon to go into the temple. Simeon took the baby Jesus in his arms and praised God,

> "Lord, I am your servant,
> and now I can die in peace,
> because you have kept
> your promise to me.
> With my own eyes I have seen
> what you have done
> to save your people,
> and foreign nations
> will also see this.

Your mighty power is a light
  for all nations,
and it will bring honor
  to your people Israel."

The Wise Men
(Matthew 2.1-12)

When Jesus was born in the village of Bethlehem in Judea, Herod was king. During this time some wise men* from the east came to Jerusalem and said, "Where is the child born to be king of the Jews? We saw his star in the east* and have come to worship him."

When King Herod heard about this, he was worried, and so was everyone else in Jerusalem. Herod brought together all the chief priests and the teachers of the Law of Moses and asked them, "Where will the Messiah be born?"

They told him, "He will be born in Bethlehem, just as the prophet wrote,

'Bethlehem in the land
  of Judea,
you are very important
  among the towns of Judea.
From your town
  will come a leader,
who will be like a shepherd
  for my people Israel.' "

Herod secretly called in the wise men and asked them when they had first seen the star. He told them, "Go to Bethlehem and search carefully for the child. As soon as you find him, let me know. I want to go and worship him too."

The wise men listened to what the king said and then left. And the star they had seen in the east went on ahead of them until it stopped over the place where the child was. They were thrilled and excited to see the star.

When the men went into the house and saw the child with Mary, his mother, they kneeled down and worshiped him. They took out their gifts of gold, frankincense, and myrrh* and gave them to him. Later they were warned in a dream not to return to Herod, and they went back home by another road.

The Boy Jesus in the Temple
(Luke 2.41-52)

Every year Jesus' parents went to Jerusalem for Passover. And when Jesus was twelve years old, they all went there as usual for the celebration. After Passover his parents left, but they did not know that Jesus had stayed on in the city. They thought he was traveling with some other people, and they went a whole day before they started looking for him. When they could not find him with their relatives and friends, they went back to Jerusalem and started looking for him there.

Three days later they found Jesus sitting in the temple, listening to the teachers and asking them questions. Everyone who heard him was surprised at how much he knew and at the questions he asked.

When his parents found him, they were amazed. His mother said, "Son, why have you done this to us? Your father and I have been very worried, and we have been searching for you!"

Jesus answered, "Why did you have to look for me? Didn't you know that I would be in my Father's house?"* But they did not understand what he meant.

Jesus went back to Nazareth with his parents and obeyed them. His mother kept on thinking about all that had happened.

Jesus became wise, and he grew strong. God was pleased with him and so were the people.

The Preaching of John the Baptist
(Matthew 3.1-11a)

Years later John the Baptist started preaching in the desert of Judea. He said, "Turn back to God! The kingdom of heaven* will soon be here."*

John was the one the prophet Isaiah was talking about, when he said,

"In the desert someone is shouting,
'Get the road ready for the Lord!
Make a straight path for him.' "

John wore clothes made of camel's hair. He had a leather strap around his waist and ate grasshoppers and wild honey.

From Jerusalem and all Judea and from the Jordan River Valley crowds of people went to John. They told how sorry they were for their sins, and he baptized them in the river.

Many Pharisees and Sadducees also came to be baptized. But John said to them:

You bunch of snakes! Who warned you to run from the coming judgment? Do something to show that you have really given up your sins. And don't start telling yourselves that you belong to Abraham's family. I tell you that God can turn these stones into children for Abraham. An ax is ready to cut the trees down at their roots. Any tree that does not produce fruit will be chopped down and thrown into a fire.

I baptize you with water so that you will give up your sins.* But someone more powerful is going to come, and I am not good enough even to carry his sandals.*

The Baptism of Jesus
(Mark 1.9-11)

About that time Jesus came from Nazareth in Galilee, and John baptized him in the Jordan River. As soon as Jesus came out of the water, he saw the sky open and the Holy Spirit coming down to him like a dove. A voice from heaven said, "You are my own dear Son, and I am pleased with you."

Jesus and the Devil
(Matthew 4.1-11)

The Holy Spirit led Jesus into the desert, so that the devil could test him. After Jesus went without eating[*] for forty days and nights, he was very hungry. Then the devil came to him and said, "If you are God's Son, tell these stones to turn into bread."

Jesus answered, "The Scriptures say:

> 'No one can live only on food.
> People need every word
>   that God has spoken.' "

Next, the devil took Jesus to the holy city and had him stand on the highest part of the temple. The devil said, "If you are God's Son, jump off. The Scriptures say:

> 'God will give his angels
>   orders about you.
> They will catch you
>   in their arms,
> and you will not hurt
>   your feet on the stones.' "

Jesus answered, "The Scriptures also say, 'Don't try to test the Lord your God!' "

Finally, the devil took Jesus up on a very high mountain and showed him all the kingdoms on earth and their power. The devil said to him, "I will give all this to you, if you will bow down and worship me."

Jesus answered, "Go away Satan! The Scriptures say:

> 'Worship the Lord your God
>   and serve only him.' "

Then the devil left Jesus, and angels came to help him.

Jesus Begins His Work
(Matthew 4.17-22; 9.9-13; 4.23-25)

Jesus started preaching, "Turn back to God! The kingdom of heaven will soon be here."*

While Jesus was walking along the shore of Lake Galilee, he saw two brothers. One was Simon, also known as Peter, and the other was Andrew. They were fishermen, and they were casting their net into the lake. Jesus said to them, "Come with me! I will teach you how to bring in people instead of fish." Right then the two brothers dropped their nets and went with him.

Jesus walked on until he saw James and John, the sons of Zebedee. They were in a boat with their father, mending their nets. Jesus asked them to come with him too. Right away they left the boat and their father and went with Jesus.

As Jesus was leaving, he saw a tax collector* named Matthew sitting at the place for paying taxes. Jesus said to him, "Come with me." Matthew got up and went with him.

Later, Jesus and his disciples were having dinner at Matthew's house.* Many tax collectors and other sinners were also there. Some Pharisees asked Jesus' disciples, "Why does your teacher eat with tax collectors and other sinners?"

Jesus heard them and answered, "Healthy people don't need a doctor, but sick people do. Go and learn what the Scriptures mean when they say, 'Instead of offering sacrifices to me, I want you to be merciful to others.' I didn't come to invite good people to be my followers. I came to invite sinners."

Jesus went all over Galilee, teaching in the Jewish meeting places and preaching the good news about God's kingdom. He also healed every kind of disease and sickness. News about him spread all over Syria, and people with every kind of sickness or disease were brought to him. Some of them had a lot of demons in them, others were thought to be crazy,* and still others could not walk. But Jesus healed them all.

Large crowds followed Jesus from Galilee and the region around the ten cities known as Decapolis.* They also came from Jerusalem, Judea, and from across the Jordan River.

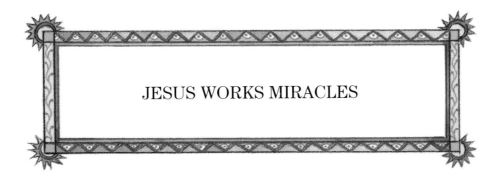

JESUS WORKS MIRACLES

Jesus Heals a Crippled Man
(Mark 2.1-12)

Jesus went back to Capernaum, and a few days later people heard that he was at home.* Then so many of them came to the house that there was not even standing room left in front of the door.

Jesus was still teaching when four people came up, carrying a crippled man on a mat. But because of the crowd, they could not get him to Jesus. So they made a hole in the roof* above him and let the man down in front of everyone.

When Jesus saw how much faith they had, he said to the crippled man, "My friend, your sins are forgiven."

Some of the teachers of the Law of Moses were sitting there. They started wondering, "Why would he say such a thing? He must think he is God! Only God can forgive sins."

Right away Jesus knew what they were thinking, and he said to them, "Why are you thinking such things? Is it easier for me to tell this crippled man that his sins are forgiven or to tell him to get up and pick up his mat and go on home? I will show you that the Son of Man has the right to forgive sins here on earth." So Jesus said to the man, "Get up! Pick up your mat and go on home."

The man got right up. He picked up his mat and went out while everyone watched in amazement. They praised God and said, "We have never seen anything like this!"

Jesus Heals an Army Officer's Servant
(Matthew 8.5-13)

When Jesus was going into the town of Capernaum, an army officer came up to him and said, "Lord, my servant is at home in such terrible pain that he can't even move."

"I will go and heal him," Jesus replied.

But the officer said, "Lord, I'm not good enough for you to come into my house. Just give the order, and my servant will get well. I have officers who give orders to me, and I have soldiers who take orders from me. I can say to one of them, 'Go!' and he goes. I can say to another, 'Come!' and he comes. I can say to my servant, 'Do this!' and he will do it."

When Jesus heard this, he was so surprised that he turned and said to the crowd following him, "I tell you that in all of Israel I've never found anyone with this much faith! Many people will come from everywhere to enjoy the feast in the kingdom of heaven with Abraham, Isaac, and Jacob. But the ones who should have been in the kingdom will be thrown out into the dark. They will cry and grit their teeth in pain."

Then Jesus said to the officer, "You may go home now. Your faith has made it happen."

Right then his servant was healed.

A Widow's Son
(Luke 7.11-17)

Soon Jesus and his disciples were on their way to the town of Nain, and a big crowd was going along with them. As they came near the gate of the town, they saw people carrying out the body of a widow's only son. Many people from the town were walking along with her.

When the Lord saw the woman, he felt sorry for her and said, "Don't cry!"

Jesus went over and touched the stretcher on which the people were carrying the dead boy. They stopped, and Jesus said, "Young man, get up!" The boy sat up and began to speak. Jesus then gave him back to his mother.

Everyone was frightened and praised God. They said, "A great prophet is here with us! God has come to his people."

News about Jesus spread all over Judea and everywhere else in that part of the country.

Ten Men with Leprosy
(Luke 17.12-19)

As Jesus was going into a village, ten men with leprosy* came toward him. They stood at a distance and shouted, "Jesus, Master, have pity on us!"

Jesus looked at them and said, "Go show yourselves to the priests."*

On their way they were healed. When one of them discovered that he was healed, he came back, shouting praises to God. He bowed down at the feet of Jesus and thanked him. The man was from the country of Samaria.

26

Jesus asked, "Weren't ten men healed? Where are the other nine? Why was this foreigner the only one who came back to thank God?" Then Jesus told the man, "You may get up and go. Your faith has made you well."

Jesus Feeds Five Thousand
(Mark 6.32-44)

Jesus and his disciples left in a boat for a place where they could be alone. But many people saw them leave and figured out where they were going. So people from every town ran on ahead and got there first.

When Jesus got out of the boat, he saw the large crowd that was like sheep without a shepherd. He felt sorry for the people and started teaching them many things.

That evening the disciples came to Jesus and said, "This place is like a desert, and it is already late. Let the crowds leave, so they can go to the farms and villages near here and buy something to eat."

Jesus replied, "You give them something to eat."

But they asked him, "Don't you know that it would take almost a year's wages* to buy all of these people something to eat?"

Then Jesus said, "How much bread do you have? Go and see!"

They found out and answered, "We have five small loaves of bread* and two fish." Jesus told his disciples to have the people sit down on the green grass. They sat down in groups of a hundred and groups of fifty.

Jesus took the five loaves and the two fish. He looked up toward heaven and blessed the food. Then he broke the bread and handed it to his disciples to give to the people. He also divided the two fish, so that everyone could have some.

After everyone had eaten all they wanted, Jesus' disciples picked up twelve large baskets of leftover bread and fish.

There were five thousand men who ate the food.

A Dying Girl and a Sick Woman
(Mark 5.21-43)

 Jesus got into the boat and crossed Lake Galilee.* Then as he stood on the shore, a large crowd gathered around him. The person in charge of the Jewish meeting place was also there. His name was Jairus, and when he saw Jesus, he went over to him. He kneeled at Jesus' feet and started begging him for help. He said, "My daughter is about to die! Please come and touch her, so she will get well and live." Jesus went with Jairus. Many people followed along and kept crowding around.

In the crowd was a woman who had been bleeding for twelve years. She had gone to many doctors, and they had not done anything except cause her a lot of pain. She had paid them all the money she had. But instead of getting better, she only got worse.

The woman had heard about Jesus, so she came up behind him in the crowd and barely touched his clothes. She had said to herself, "If I can just touch his clothes, I will get well." As soon as she touched them, her bleeding stopped, and she knew she was well.

At that moment Jesus felt power go out from him. He turned to the crowd and asked, "Who touched my clothes?"

His disciples said to him, "Look at all these people crowding around you! How can you ask who touched you?" But Jesus turned to see who had touched him.

The woman knew what had happened to her. She came shaking with fear and kneeled down in front of Jesus. Then she told him the whole story.

Jesus said to the woman, "You are now well because of your faith. May God give you peace! You are healed, and you will no longer be in pain."

While Jesus was still speaking, some men came from Jairus' home and said, "Your daughter has died! Why bother the teacher anymore?"

Jesus heard* what they said, and he said to Jairus, "Don't worry. Just have faith!"

Jesus did not let anyone go with him except Peter and the two brothers, James and John. They went home with Jairus and saw the people crying and making a lot of noise.* Then Jesus went inside and said to them, "Why are you crying and carrying on like this? The child is not dead. She is just asleep." But the people laughed at him.

After Jesus had sent them all out of the house, he took the girl's father and mother and his three disciples and went to where she was. He took the twelve-year-old girl by the hand and said, "Talitha, koum!"* which means, "Little girl, get up!" The girl got right up and started walking around.

Everyone was greatly surprised. But Jesus ordered them not to tell anyone what had happened. Then he said, "Give her something to eat."

A Man with Evil Spirits
(Mark 5.1-20)

Jesus and his disciples crossed Lake Galilee and came to shore near the town of Gerasa.* When he was getting out of the boat, a man with an evil spirit quickly ran to him from the graveyard* where he had been living. No one was able to tie the man up anymore, not even with a chain. He had often been put in chains and leg irons, but he broke the chains and smashed the leg irons. No one could control him. Night and day he was in the graveyard or on the hills, yelling and cutting himself with stones.

When the man saw Jesus in the distance, he ran up to him and kneeled down. He shouted, "Jesus, Son of God in heaven, what do you want with me? Promise me in God's name that you won't torture me!" The man said this because Jesus had already told the evil spirit to come out of him.

Jesus asked him, "What is your name?"

The man answered, "My name is Lots, because I have 'lots' of evil spirits." He then begged Jesus not to send him away.

Over on the hillside a large herd of pigs was feeding. So the evil spirits begged Jesus, "Send us into those pigs! Let us go into them." Jesus let them go, and they went out of the man and into the pigs. The whole herd of about two

thousand pigs rushed down the steep bank into the lake and drowned.

The men taking care of the pigs ran to the town and the farms to spread the news. Then the people came out to see what had happened. When they came to Jesus, they saw the man who had once been full of demons. He was sitting there with his clothes on and in his right mind, and they were terrified.

Everyone who had seen what had happened told about the man and the pigs. Then the people started begging Jesus to leave their part of the country.

When Jesus was getting into the boat, the man begged to go with him. But Jesus would not let him. Instead, he said, "Go home to your family and tell them how much the Lord has done for you and how good he has been to you."

The man went away into the region near the ten cities known as Decapolis* and began telling everyone how much Jesus had done for him. Everyone who heard what happened was amazed.

JESUS HELPS PEOPLE

Simon the Pharisee
(Luke 7.36-50)

A Pharisee invited Jesus to have dinner with him. So Jesus went to the Pharisee's home and got ready to eat.*

When a sinful woman in that town found out that Jesus was there, she bought an expensive bottle of perfume. Then she came and stood behind Jesus. She cried and started washing his feet with her tears and drying them with her hair. The woman kissed his feet and poured the perfume on them.

The Pharisee who had invited Jesus saw this and said to himself, "If this man really were a prophet, he would know what

kind of woman is touching him! He would know that she
is a sinner."

Jesus said to the Pharisee, "Simon, I have something
to say to you."

"Teacher, what is it?" Simon replied.

Jesus told him, "Two people were in debt to a moneylender.
One of them owed him five hundred silver coins, and the other
owed him fifty. Since neither of them could pay him back, the
moneylender said that they didn't have to pay him anything.
Which one of them will like him more?"

Simon answered, "I suppose it would be the one who had
owed more and didn't have to pay it back."

"You are right," Jesus said.

He turned toward the woman and said to Simon, "Have you
noticed this woman? When I came into your home, you didn't give
me any water so I could wash my feet. But she has washed my feet
with her tears and dried them with her hair. You didn't greet me
with a kiss, but from the time I came in, she has not stopped
kissing my feet. You didn't even pour olive oil on my head,* but she
has poured expensive perfume on my feet. So I tell you that all her
sins are forgiven, and that is why she has shown great love. But
anyone who has been forgiven only a little will show only a little
love."

Then Jesus said to the woman, "Your sins are forgiven."

Some other guests started saying to one another, "Who is
this who dares to forgive sins?"

But Jesus told the woman, "Because of your faith, you are
now saved.* May God give you peace!"

A Rich Man
(Mark 10.17-27)

As Jesus was walking down a road, a man ran up to him. He kneeled down, and asked, "Good teacher, what can I do to have eternal life?"

Jesus replied, "Why do you call me good? Only God is good. You know the commandments. 'Do not murder. Be faithful in marriage. Do not steal. Do not tell lies about others. Do not cheat. Respect your father and mother.' "

The man answered, "Teacher, I have obeyed all these commandments since I was a young man."

Jesus looked closely at the man. He liked him and said, "There's one thing you still need to do. Go sell everything you own. Give the money to the poor, and you will have riches in heaven. Then come with me."

When the man heard Jesus say this, he went away gloomy and sad because he was very rich.

Jesus looked around and said to his disciples, "It's hard for rich people to get into God's kingdom!" The disciples were shocked to hear this. So Jesus told them again, "It's terribly hard* to get into God's kingdom! In fact, it's easier for a camel to go through the eye of a needle than for a rich person to get into God's kingdom."

Jesus' disciples were even more amazed. They asked each other, "How can anyone ever be saved?"

Jesus looked at them and said, "There are some things that people cannot do, but God can do anything."

Martha and Mary
(Luke 10.38-42)

The Lord and his disciples were traveling along and came to a village. When they got there, a woman named Martha welcomed him into her home. She had a sister named Mary, who sat down in front of the Lord and was listening to what he said. Martha was worried about all that had to be done. Finally, she went to Jesus and said, "Lord, doesn't it bother you that my sister has left me to do all the work by myself? Tell her to come and help me!"

The Lord answered, "Martha, Martha! You are worried and upset about so many things, but only one thing is necessary. Mary has chosen what is best, and it will not be taken away from her."

Zacchaeus
(Luke 19.1-10)

Jesus was going through Jericho, where a man named Zacchaeus lived. He was in charge of collecting taxes* and was very rich. Jesus was heading his way, and Zacchaeus wanted to see what he was like. But Zacchaeus was a short man and could not see over the crowd. So he ran ahead and climbed up into a sycamore tree.

When Jesus got there, he looked up and said, "Zacchaeus, hurry down! I want to stay with you today." Zacchaeus hurried down and gladly welcomed Jesus.

Everyone who saw this started grumbling, "This man Zacchaeus is a sinner! And Jesus is going home to eat with him."

Later that day Zacchaeus stood up and said to the Lord, "I will give half of my property to the poor. And I will now pay back four times as much* to everyone I have ever cheated."

Jesus said to Zacchaeus, "Today you and your family have been saved,* because you are a true son of Abraham.* The Son of Man came to look for and to save people who are lost."

JESUS TEACHES

The Good Samaritan
(Luke 10.25-37)

An expert in the Law of Moses stood up and asked Jesus a question to see what he would say. "Teacher," he asked, "What must I do to have eternal life?"

Jesus answered, "What is written in the Scriptures? How do you understand them?"

The man replied, "The Scriptures say, 'Love the Lord your God with all your heart, soul, strength, and mind.' They also say, 'Love your neighbors as much as you love yourself.' "

Jesus said, "You have given the right answer. If you do this, you will have eternal life."

But the man wanted to show that he knew what he was talking about. So he asked Jesus, "Who are my neighbors?"

Jesus replied:

As a man was going down from Jerusalem to Jericho, robbers attacked him and grabbed everything he had. They beat him up and ran off, leaving him half dead.

A priest happened to be going down the same road. But when he saw the man, he walked by on the other side. Later a temple helper* came to the same place. But when he saw the man who had been beaten up, he also went by on the other side.

A man from Samaria then came traveling along that road. When he saw the man, he felt sorry for him and went over to him. He treated his wounds with olive oil and wine[*] and bandaged them. Then he put him on his own donkey and took him to an inn, where he took care of him. The next morning he gave the innkeeper two silver coins and said, "Please take care of the man. If you spend more than this on him, I will pay you when I return."

Then Jesus asked, "Which one of these three people was a real neighbor to the man who was beaten up by robbers?"

The teacher answered, "The one who showed pity."

Jesus said, "Go and do the same!"

A Rich Fool
(Luke 12.13-21)

A man in a crowd said to Jesus, "Teacher, tell my brother to give me my share of what our father left us when he died."

Jesus answered, "Who gave me the right to settle arguments between you and your brother?"

Then he said to the crowd, "Don't be greedy! Owning a lot of things won't make your life safe."

So Jesus told them this story:

A rich man's farm produced a big crop, and he said to himself, "What can I do? I don't have a place large enough to store everything."

Later, he said, "Now I know what I'll do. I'll tear down my barns and build bigger ones, where I can store all my grain and other goods. Then I'll say to myself, 'You have stored up enough good things to last for years to come. Live it up! Eat, drink, and enjoy yourself.' "

But God said to him, "You fool! Tonight you will die. Then who will get what you have stored up?"

"This is what happens to people who store up everything for themselves, but are poor in the sight of God."

One Sheep
(Luke 15.1-7)

Tax collectors* and sinners were all crowding around to listen to Jesus. So the Pharisees and the teachers of the Law of Moses started grumbling, "This man is friendly with sinners. He even eats with them."

Then Jesus told them this story:

> If any of you has a hundred sheep, and one of them gets lost, what will you do? Won't you leave the ninety-nine in the field and go look for the lost sheep until you find it? And when you find it, you will be so glad that you will put it on your shoulder and carry it home. Then you will call in your friends and neighbors and say, "Let's celebrate! I've found my lost sheep."

Jesus said, "In the same way there is more happiness in heaven because of one sinner who turns to God than over ninety-nine good people who don't need to."

One Coin
(Luke 15.8-10)

Jesus told the people another story:

What will a woman do if she has ten silver coins and loses one of them? Won't she light a lamp, sweep the floor, and look carefully until she finds it? Then she will call in her friends and neighbors and say,

"Let's celebrate! I've found the coin I lost."

Jesus said, "In the same way God's angels are happy when even one person turns to him."

Two Sons
(Luke 15.11-32)

Jesus also told them another story:

Once a man had two sons. The younger son said to his father, "Give me my share of the property." So the father divided his property between his two sons.

Not long after that, the younger son packed up everything he owned and left for a foreign country, where he wasted all his money in wild living. He had spent everything, when a bad famine spread through that whole land. Soon he had nothing to eat.

He went to work for a man in that country, and the man sent him out to take care of his pigs.* He would have been glad to eat what the pigs were eating,* but no one gave him a thing.

Finally, he came to his senses and said, "My father's workers have plenty to eat, and here I am, starving to death! I will leave and go to my father and say to him, 'Father, I have sinned against God in heaven and against you. I am no longer good enough to be called your son. Treat me like one of your workers.' "

The younger son got up and started back to his father. But when he was still a long way off, his father saw him and felt sorry for him. He ran to his son and hugged and kissed him.

The son said, "Father, I have sinned against God in heaven and against you. I am no longer good enough to be called your son."

But his father said to the servants, "Hurry and bring the best clothes and put them on him. Give him a ring for his finger and sandals* for his feet. Get the best calf and prepare it, so we can eat and celebrate. This son of mine was dead, but has now come back to life. He was lost and has now been found." And they began to celebrate.

The older son had been out in the field. But when he came near the house, he heard the music and dancing. So he called one of the servants over and asked, "What's going on here?"

The servant answered, "Your brother has come home safe and sound, and your father ordered us to kill the best calf." The older brother got so mad that he would not even go into the house.

His father came out and begged him to go in. But he said to his father, "For years I have worked for you like a slave and have always obeyed you. But you have never even given me a little goat, so that I could give a dinner for my friends. This other son of yours wasted your money on bad women. And now that he has come home, you ordered the best calf to be killed for a feast."

His father replied, "My son, you are always with me, and everything I have is yours. But we should be glad and celebrate! Your brother was dead, but he is now alive. He was lost and has now been found."

Prayer
(Matthew 6.5-15)

When you pray, don't be like those showoffs who love to stand up and pray in the meeting places and on the street corners. They do this just to look good. I promise you that they already have their reward.

When you pray, go into a room alone and close the door. Pray to your Father in private. He knows what is done in private, and he will reward you.

When you pray, don't talk on and on as people do who don't know God. They think God likes to hear long prayers. Don't be like them. Your Father knows what you need before you ask.

You should pray like this:
Our Father in heaven,
   help us to honor your name.
Come and set up your kingdom,
so that everyone on earth
   will obey you,
as you are obeyed
   in heaven.
Give us our food for today.*
Forgive our sins,
   as we forgive others.*
Keep us from being tempted
   and protect us from evil.*

If you forgive others for the wrongs they do to you, your Father in heaven will forgive you. But if you don't forgive others, your Father will not forgive your sins.

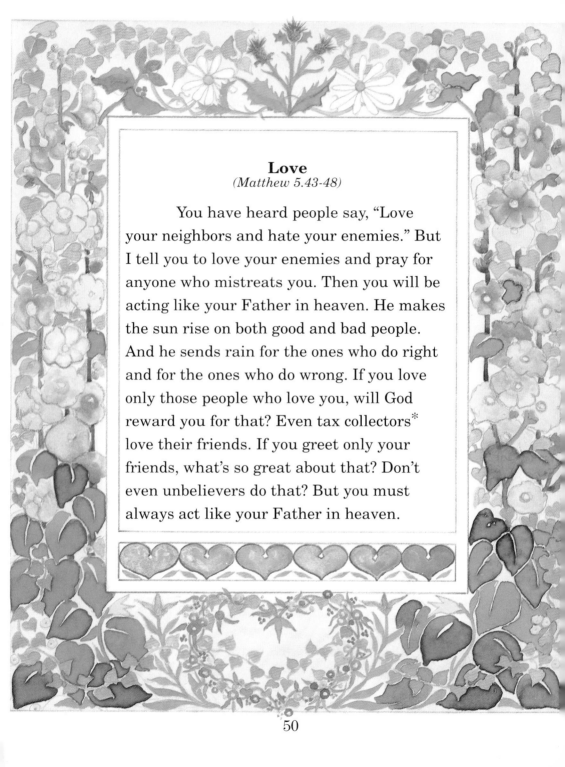

Love
(Matthew 5.43-48)

You have heard people say, "Love your neighbors and hate your enemies." But I tell you to love your enemies and pray for anyone who mistreats you. Then you will be acting like your Father in heaven. He makes the sun rise on both good and bad people. And he sends rain for the ones who do right and for the ones who do wrong. If you love only those people who love you, will God reward you for that? Even tax collectors* love their friends. If you greet only your friends, what's so great about that? Don't even unbelievers do that? But you must always act like your Father in heaven.

Giving
(Matthew 6.1-4)

When you do good deeds, don't try to show off. If you do, you won't get a reward from your Father in heaven.

When you give to the poor, don't blow a loud horn. That's what showoffs do in the meeting places and on the street corners, because they are always looking for praise. I promise you that they already have their reward.

When you give to the poor, don't let anyone know about it.* Then your gift will be given in secret. Your Father knows what is done in secret, and he will reward you.

Worry
(Matthew 6.25-34)

I tell you not to worry about your life. Don't worry about having something to eat, drink, or wear. Isn't life more than food or clothing? Look at the birds in the sky! They don't plant or harvest. They don't even store grain in barns. Yet your Father in heaven takes care of them. Aren't you worth more than birds?

Can worry make you live longer?* Why worry about clothes? Look how the wild flowers grow. They don't work hard to make their clothes. But I tell you that Solomon with all his wealth* was not as well clothed as one of them. God gives such beauty to everything that grows in the fields, even though it is here today and thrown into a fire tomorrow. He will surely do even more for you! Why do you have such little faith?

Don't worry and ask yourselves, "Will we have anything to eat? Will we have anything to drink? Will we have any clothes to wear?" Only people who don't know God are always worrying about such things. Your Father in heaven knows that you need all of these. But more than anything else, put God's work first and do what he wants. Then all the other things will be yours as well.

Don't worry about tomorrow. It will take care of itself. You have enough to worry about today.

THE END AND THE NEW BEGINNING

The Plot to Kill Jesus
(Matthew 26.1-5)

When Jesus had finished teaching, he told his disciples, "You know that two days from now will be Passover. That is when the Son of Man will be handed over to his enemies and nailed to a cross."

At that time the chief priests and the nation's leaders were meeting at the home of Caiaphas the high priest. They planned how they could sneak around and have Jesus arrested and put to death. But they said, "We must not do it during Passover, because the people will riot."

At Bethany
(Matthew 26.6-13)

Jesus was in the town of Bethany, eating at the home of Simon, who once had leprosy.* A woman came in with a bottle of expensive perfume and poured it on Jesus' head. But when his disciples saw this, they became angry. They said, "Why such a waste? We could have sold this perfume for a lot of money and given it to the poor."

Jesus knew what they were thinking, and he said:

Why are you bothering this woman? She has done a beautiful thing for me. You will always have the poor with you, but you will not always have me. She has poured perfume on my body to prepare it for burial.* You may be sure that wherever the good news is told all over the world, people will remember what she has done. And they will tell others.

Judas and the Chief Priests
(Matthew 26.14-16)

Judas Iscariot* was one of the twelve disciples. He went to the chief priests and asked, "How much will you give me if I help you arrest Jesus?" They paid Judas thirty silver coins, and from then on he started looking for a good chance to betray Jesus.

Jesus Eats the Passover Meal with His Disciples
(Matthew 26.17-30)

On the first day of the Feast of Thin Bread, Jesus' disciples came to him and asked, "Where do you want us to prepare the Passover meal?"

Jesus told them to go to a certain man in the city and tell him, "Our teacher says, 'My time has come! I want to eat the Passover meal with my disciples in your home.' " They did as Jesus told them and prepared the meal.

When Jesus was eating with his twelve disciples that evening, he said, "One of you will surely hand me over to my enemies."

The disciples were very sad, and each one said to Jesus, "Surely, Lord, you don't mean me!"

He answered, "One of you men who has eaten with me from this dish will betray me. The Son of Man will die, as the Scriptures say. But it's going to be terrible for the one who betrays me! That man would be better off if he had never been born."

Judas said, "Teacher, surely you don't mean me!"

"That's what you say!" Jesus replied. But later, Judas did betray him.

During the meal Jesus took some bread in his hands. He blessed the bread and broke it. Then he gave it to his disciples and said, "Take this and eat it. This is my body."

Jesus picked up a cup of wine and gave thanks to God. He then gave it to his disciples and said, "Take this and drink it. This is my blood, and with it God makes his agreement with you. It will be poured out, so that many people will have their sins forgiven. From now on I am not going to drink any wine, until I drink new wine with you in my Father's kingdom." Then they sang a hymn and went out to the Mount of Olives.

Peter's Promise
(Matthew 26.31-35)

Jesus said to his disciples, "During this very night, all of you will reject me, as the Scriptures say,

    'I will strike down
        the shepherd,
    and the sheep
        will be scattered.'

But after I am raised to life, I will go to Galilee ahead of you."

Peter spoke up, "Even if all the others reject you, I never will!"

Jesus replied, "I promise you that before a rooster crows tonight, you will say three times that you don't know me." But Peter said, "Even if I have to die with you, I will never say I don't know you."

All the others said the same thing.

Jesus Prays
(Matthew 26.36-46)

Jesus went with his disciples to a place called Gethsemane. When they got there, he told them, "Sit here while I go over there and pray."

Jesus took along Peter and the two brothers, James and John.* He was very sad and troubled, and he said to them, "I am so sad that I feel as if I am dying. Stay here and keep awake with me."

Jesus walked on a little way. Then he kneeled with his face to the ground and prayed, "My Father, if it is possible, don't make me suffer by having me drink from this cup.* But do what you want, and not what I want."

He came back and found his disciples sleeping. So he said to Peter, "Can't any of you stay awake with me for just one hour? Stay awake and pray that you will not be tested. You want to do what is right, but you are weak."

Again Jesus went to pray and said, "My Father, if there is no other way, and I must suffer, I will still do what you want."

Jesus came back and found them sleeping again. They simply could not keep their eyes open. He left them and prayed the same prayer once more.

Finally, Jesus returned to his disciples and said, "Are you still sleeping and resting?* The time has come for the Son of Man to be handed over to sinners. Get up! Let's go. The one who will betray me is already here."

Jesus Is Arrested
(Matthew 26.47-56)

 Jesus was still speaking, when Judas the betrayer came up. He was one of the twelve disciples, and a large mob armed with swords and clubs was with him. They had been sent by the chief priests and the nation's leaders. Judas had told them ahead of time, "Arrest the man I greet with a kiss."*

Judas walked right up to Jesus and said, "Hello, teacher." Then Judas kissed him.

Jesus replied, "My friend, why are you here?"*

The men grabbed Jesus and arrested him. One of Jesus' followers pulled out a sword. He struck the servant of the high priest and cut off his ear.

But Jesus told him, "Put your sword away. Anyone who lives by fighting will die by fighting. Don't you know that I could ask my Father, and right away he would send me more than twelve armies of angels? But then, how could the words of the Scriptures come true, which say that this must happen?"

Jesus said to the mob, "Why do you come with swords and clubs to arrest me like a criminal? Day after day I sat and taught in the temple, and you didn't arrest me. But all this happened, so that what the prophets wrote would come true."

All of Jesus' disciples left him and ran away.

Jesus Is Questioned by the Jewish Council
(Matthew 26.57-68)

After Jesus had been arrested, he was led off to the house of Caiaphas the high priest. The nation's leaders and the teachers of the Law of Moses were meeting there. But Peter followed along at a distance and came to the courtyard of the high priest's palace. He went in and sat down with the guards to see what was going to happen.

The chief priests and the whole council wanted to put Jesus to death. So they tried to find some people who would tell lies about him in court.* But they could not find any, even though many did come and tell lies. At last two men came forward and said, "This man claimed that he would tear down God's temple and build it again in three days."

The high priest stood up and asked Jesus, "Why don't you say something in your own defense? Don't you hear the charges they are making against you?" But Jesus did not answer. So the high priest said, "With the living God looking on, you must tell the truth. Tell us, are you the Messiah, the Son of God?"*

"That is what you say!" Jesus answered. "But I tell all of you,

'Soon you will see
the Son of Man
sitting at the right side*
of God All-Powerful
and coming on the clouds
of heaven.' "

The high priest then tore his robe and said, "This man claims to be God! We don't need any more witnesses! You have heard what he said. What do you think?"

They answered, "He is guilty and deserves to die!" Then they spit in his face and hit him with their fists. Others slapped him and said, "You think you are the Messiah! So tell us who hit you!"

Peter Says He Does Not Know Jesus
(Matthew 26.69-75)

While Peter was sitting out in the courtyard, a servant girl came up to him and said, "You were with Jesus from Galilee."

But in front of everyone Peter said, "That's not so! I don't know what you are talking about!"

When Peter had gone out to the gate, another servant girl saw him and said to some people there, "This man was with Jesus from Nazareth."

Again Peter denied it, and this time he swore, "I don't even know that man!"

A little while later some people standing there walked over to Peter and said, "We know that you are one of them. We can tell it because you talk like someone from Galilee."

Peter began to curse and swear, "I don't know that man!"

Right then a rooster crowed, and Peter remembered that Jesus had said, "Before a rooster crows, you will say three times that you don't know me." Then Peter went out and cried hard.

Jesus Is Taken to Pilate
(Matthew 27.1-2)

Early the next morning all the chief priests and the nation's leaders met and decided that Jesus should be put to death. They tied him up and led him away to Pilate the governor.

The Death of Judas
(Matthew 27.3-10)

When Judas learned that Jesus had been sentenced to death, he was sorry for what he had done. He returned the thirty silver coins to the chief priests and leaders and said, "I have sinned by betraying a man who has never done anything wrong."

"So what? That's your problem," they replied. Judas threw the money into the temple and then went out and hanged himself.

The chief priests picked up the money and said, "This money was paid to have a man killed. We can't put it in the temple treasury." Then they had a meeting and decided to buy a field that belonged to someone who made clay pots. They wanted to use it as a graveyard for foreigners. That is why people still call that place "Field of Blood." So the words of the prophet Jeremiah came true,

> "They took
>> the thirty silver coins,
>
> the price of a person
>> among the people of Israel.
>
> They paid it
>> for a potter's field,*
>
> as the Lord
>> had commanded me."

Pilate Questions Jesus
(Matthew 27.11-14)

Jesus was brought before Pilate the governor, who asked him, "Are you the King of the Jews?"

"Those are your words!" Jesus answered. And when the chief priests and leaders brought their charges against him, he did not say a thing.

Pilate asked him, "Don't you hear what crimes they say you have done?" But Jesus did not say anything, and the governor was greatly amazed.

The Death Sentence
(Matthew 27.15-26)

During Passover the governor always freed a prisoner chosen by the people. At that time a well-known terrorist named Jesus Barabbas* was in jail. So when the crowd came together, Pilate asked them, "Which prisoner do you want me to set free? Do you want Jesus Barabbas or Jesus who is called the Messiah?" Pilate knew that the leaders had brought Jesus to him because they were jealous.

While Pilate was judging the case, his wife sent him a message. It said, "Don't have anything to do with that innocent man. I have had nightmares because of him."

But the chief priests and the leaders convinced the crowds to ask for Barabbas to be set free and for Jesus to be killed. Pilate asked the crowd again, "Which of these two men do you want me to set free?"

"Barabbas!" they replied.

Pilate asked them, "What am I to do with Jesus, who is called the Messiah?"

They all yelled, "Nail him to a cross!"

Pilate answered, "But what crime has he done?"

"Nail him to a cross!" they yelled even louder.

Pilate saw that there was nothing he could do and that the people were starting to riot. So he took some water and washed his hands* in front of them and said, "I won't have anything to do with killing this man. You are the ones doing it!"

Everyone answered, "We and our descendants will take the blame for his death!"

Pilate set Barabbas free. Then he ordered his soldiers to beat Jesus with a whip and nail him to a cross.

Soldiers Make Fun of Jesus
(Matthew 27.27-32)

The governor's soldiers led Jesus into the fortress* and brought together the rest of the troops. They stripped off Jesus' clothes and put a scarlet robe* on him. They made a crown out of thorn branches and placed it on his head, and they put a stick in his right hand. The soldiers kneeled down and pretended to worship him. They made fun of him and shouted, "Hey, you king of the Jews!" Then they spit on him. They took the stick from him and beat him on the head with it.

When the soldiers had finished making fun of Jesus, they took off the robe. They put his own clothes back on him and led him off to be nailed to a cross. On the way they met a man from Cyrene named Simon, and they forced him to carry Jesus' cross.

Jesus Is Nailed to a Cross
(Matthew 27.33-44)

They came to a place named Golgotha, which means "Place of the Skull."* There they gave Jesus some wine mixed with a drug to ease the pain. But when Jesus tasted what it was, he refused to drink it.

The soldiers nailed Jesus to a cross and gambled to see who would get his clothes. They they sat down to guard him. Above his head they put a sign that told why he was nailed there. It read, "This is Jesus, the King of the Jews." The soldiers also nailed two criminals on crosses, one to the right of Jesus and the other to his left.

People who passed by said terrible things about Jesus. They shook their heads and shouted, "So you're the one who claimed you could tear down the temple and build it again in three days! If you are God's Son, save yourself and come down from the cross!"

The chief priests, the leaders, and the teachers of the Law of Moses also made fun of Jesus. They said, "He saved others, but he can't save himself. If he is the king of Israel, he should come down from the cross! Then we will believe him. He trusted God, so let God save him, if he wants to. He even said he was God's Son." The two criminals also said cruel things to Jesus.

The Death of Jesus
(Matthew 27.45-56)

At noon the sky turned dark and stayed that way until three o'clock. Then about that time Jesus shouted, "Eli, Eli, lema sabachthani?"* which means, "My God, my God, why have you deserted me?"

Some of the people standing there heard Jesus and said, "He's calling for Elijah."* One of them at once ran and grabbed a sponge. He soaked it in wine, then put it on a stick and held it up to Jesus.

Others said, "Wait! Let's see if Elijah will come* and save him." Once again Jesus shouted, and then he died.

At once the curtain in the temple* was torn in two from top to bottom. The earth shook, and rocks split apart. Graves opened, and many of God's people were raised to life. Then after Jesus had risen to life, they came out of their graves and went into the holy city, where many people saw them.

The officer and the soldiers guarding Jesus felt the earthquake and saw everything else that happened. They were frightened and said, "This man really was God's Son!"

Many women were looking on from a distance. They had come with Jesus from Galilee to be of help to him. Mary Magdalene, Mary the mother of James and Joseph, and the mother of James and John* were some of these women.

Jesus Is Buried
(Matthew 27.57-66)

That evening a rich disciple named Joseph from the town of Arimathea went and asked for Jesus' body. Pilate gave orders for it to be given to Joseph, who took the body and wrapped it in a clean linen cloth. Then Joseph put the body in his own tomb that had been cut into solid rock* and had never been used. He rolled a big stone against the entrance to the tomb and went away.

All this time Mary Magdalene and the other Mary were sitting across from the tomb.

On the next day, which was a Sabbath, the chief priests and the Pharisees went together to Pilate. They said, "Sir, we remember what that liar said while he was still alive. He claimed that in three days he would come back from death. So please order the tomb to be carefully guarded for three days. If you don't, his disciples may come and steal his body. They will tell people that he has been raised to life, and this last lie will be worse than the first one."*

Pilate said to them, "All right, take some of your soldiers and guard the tomb as well as you know how." So they sealed it tight and placed soldiers there to guard it.

Jesus Is Alive
(Matthew 28.1-10)

The Sabbath was over, and it was almost daybreak on Sunday when Mary Magdalene and the other Mary went to see the tomb. Suddenly a strong earthquake struck, and the Lord's angel came down from heaven. He rolled away the stone and sat on it. The angel looked as bright as lightning, and his clothes were white as snow. The guards shook from fear and fell down, as though they were dead.

The angel said to the women, "Don't be afraid! I know you are looking for Jesus, who was nailed to a cross. He is not here! God has raised him to life, just as Jesus said he would. Come, see the place where his body was lying. Now hurry! Tell his disciples that he has been raised to life and is on his way to Galilee. Go there, and you will see him. That is what I came to tell you."

The women were frightened and yet very happy, as they hurried from the tomb and ran to tell his disciples. Suddenly Jesus met them and greeted them. They went near to him, held on to his feet, and worshiped him. Jesus said to them, "Don't be afraid! Tell my followers to go to Galilee. They will see me there."

Report of the Guard
(Matthew 28.11-15)

While the women were on their way, some soldiers who had been guarding the tomb went into the city. They told the chief priests everything that had happened. So the chief priests met with the leaders and decided to bribe the soldiers with a lot of money. They said to the soldiers, "Tell everyone that Jesus' disciples came during the night and stole his body while you were asleep. If the governor* hears about this, we will talk to him. You won't have anything to worry about." The soldiers took the money and did what they were told. The Jewish people still tell each other this story.

What Jesus' Followers Must Do
(Matthew 28.16-20)

Jesus' eleven disciples went to a mountain in Galilee, where Jesus had told them to meet him. They saw him and worshiped him, but some of them doubted.

Jesus came to them and said:

I have been given all authority in heaven and on earth! Go to the people of all nations and make them my disciples. Baptize them in the name of the Father, the Son, and the Holy Spirit, and teach them to do everything I have told you. I will be with you always, even until the end of the world.

SPECIAL HELPS

IMPORTANT WORDS TO KNOW

chief priests: See "priest."

Christ: A Greek word meaning "the Chosen One" and used to translate the Hebrew word "Messiah."

commandments: God's rules for his people to live by.

council: A leading group of Jewish men who were allowed by the Roman government to meet and make certain decisions for their people.

Decapolis: A group of ten towns. Most of the people who lived there were not Jews.

demons and **evil spirits:** Supernatural beings that do harmful things to people and sometimes cause them to do bad things. In the New Testament they are sometimes called "unclean spirits," because people under their power were thought to be unclean and unfit to worship God.

devil: The chief of the demons and evil spirits, also known as "Satan."

disciple: Someone who was a follower of Jesus and learned from him.

Emperor: The ruler who lived in the city of Rome and governed all the land around the Mediterranean Sea.

Feast of Thin Bread: The days after Passover when Jews ate a kind of thin, flat bread made without yeast. See "Passover."

feed box: A place where animals were fed hay and grain.

frankincense: A valuable powder that was burned to make a sweet smell.

God's kingdom: God's rule over people, both in this life and in the next. In the Gospel of Matthew "Kingdom of heaven" is used with the same meaning as "God's kingdom" in Mark and Luke.

high priest: See "priest."

holy city: Jerusalem.

Jewish meeting place: A place where Jews met to read and study their Bible and to worship.

kingdom of heaven: See "God's kingdom."

Law of Moses and **Law of the Lord:** Usually refers to the first five books of the Old Testament, but sometimes to the entire Old Testament.

leprosy: In biblical times the word "leprosy" was used for many different kinds of skin diseases.

Messiah: See "Christ."

myrrh: A valuable sweet-smelling powder often used in perfume.

Passover: A day each year in the spring when Jews celebrate the time God rescued them from slavery in Egypt.

Pharisees: A large group of Jews who thought they could best serve God by strictly obeying the laws of the Old Testament as well as their own teachings.

priest: A man who led the worship in the temple and offered sacrifices. Some of the more important priests were called "chief priests," and the most important priest was called "high priest."

Sabbath: The seventh day of the week when Jews worship and do not work, in obedience to the third commandment.

Sadducees: A small and powerful group of Jews who were closely connected with the high priests and who accepted only the first five books of the Old Testament as their Bible. They also did not believe in life after death.

Samaria: A district between Judea and Galilee. The people of Samaria, called Samaritans, worshiped God differently from the Jews and did not get along with them.

Satan: See "devil."

save: To rescue people from the power of evil, to give them new life, and to place them under God's care. See "Savior."

Savior: The one who rescues people from the power of evil, gives them new life, and places them under God's care. See "save."

Son of Man: A name often used by Jesus to refer to himself. It is also found in the book of Daniel and refers to the one to whom God has given the power to rule.

taxes and **tax collectors:** Special fees collected by rulers, usually part of the value of a citizen's crops, property, or income. There were also market taxes to be paid, and customs taxes were collected at ports and border crossings. The wealthy Zacchaeus (Luke 19.1-10) was a tax collector who collected taxes at a border crossing near Jericho. Jews hired by the Roman government to collect taxes from other Jews were hated by their own people.

temple: A building used as a place of worship. The Jewish temple was in Jerusalem.

wise men: Men famous for their study of the stars.

(*)NOTES

(Page 9) **good man:** Or "kind man," or "man who always did the right thing."

(Page 9) **name him Jesus:** In Hebrew the name "Jesus" means "the Lord saves."

(Page 9) **names . . . listed in record books:** This was done so that everyone could be made to pay taxes to the Emperor.

(Page 9) **Quirinius was governor of Syria:** It is known that Quirinius made a record of the people in A.D. 6 or 7. But the exact date of the record taking that Luke mentions is not known.

(Page 9) **first-born:** The Jewish people said that the first-born son in each of their families belonged to God.

(Page 10) **dressed in baby clothes:** The Greek text was "wrapped him in wide strips of cloth," which was how young babies were dressed.

(Page 12) **after her baby is born:** After a Jewish mother gave birth to a son, she was considered "unclean" and had to stay home until he was circumcised. She then had to stay home for another 33 days, before offering a sacrifice to the Lord.

(Page 12) **first-born:** See the note on page 9.

(Page 14) **wise men:** People famous for studying the stars.

(Page 14) **his star in the east:** Or "his star rise."

(Page 15) **frankincense, and myrrh:** Frankincense was a valuable powder that was burned to make a sweet smell. Myrrh was a valuable sweet-smelling powder often used in perfume.

(Page 16) **in my Father's house:** Or "doing my Father's work."

(Page 17) **kingdom of heaven:** In the Gospel of Matthew "kingdom of heaven" is used with the same meaning as "God's kingdom" in Mark and Luke.

(Page 17) **will soon be here:** Or "is already here."

(Page 17) **so that you will give up your sins:** Or "because you have given up your sins."

(Page 17) **carry his sandals:** This was one of the duties of a slave.

(Page 18) **went without eating:** The Jewish people sometimes went without eating (also called "fasting") to show their love for God and to become better followers.

(Page 20) **The kingdom of heaven will soon be here:** See the note on page 17.

(Page 20) **tax collector:** These were usually Jewish people who paid the Romans for the right to collect taxes. They were hated by other Jews who thought of them as traitors to their country and to their religion.

(Page 21) **Matthew's house:** Or "Jesus' house."

(Page 21) **thought to be crazy:** In ancient times people with epilepsy were thought to be crazy.

(Page 21) **the ten cities known as Decapolis:** A group of ten cities east of Samaria and Galilee, where the people followed the Greek way of life.

(Page 24) **at home:** Or "in the house" (perhaps Simon Peter's home).

(Page 24) **roof:** In Palestine the houses usually had a flat roof. Stairs on the outside led up to the roof that was made of beams and boards covered with packed earth.

(Page 26) **leprosy:** In biblical times the word "leprosy" was used for many different skin diseases.

(Page 26) **show yourselves to the priests:** People with leprosy had to be examined by a priest and told that they were well (that is "clean") before they could once again live a normal life in the Jewish community.

(Page 27) **almost a year's wages:** The Greek text has "two hundred silver coins." Each coin was the average day's wage for a worker.

(Page 28) **small loaves of bread:** These would have been flat and round or in the shape of a bun.

(Page 28) **crossed Lake Galilee:** To the west side.

(Page 30) **heard:** Or "ignored."

(Page 30) **crying and making a lot of noise:** The Jewish people often hired mourners for funerals.

(Page 30) **Talitha, koum:** These words are in Aramaic, a language spoken in Palestine during the time of Jesus.

(Page 31) **Gerasa:** Some manuscripts have "Gadara," and others have "Gergesa."

(Page 31) **graveyard:** It was thought that demons and evil spirits lived in graveyards.

(Page 32) **the ten cities known as Decapolis:** See the note on page 21.

(Page 34) **got ready to eat:** On special occasions the Jewish people often followed the Greek and Roman custom of lying down on their left side and leaning on their left elbow, while eating with their right hand. This is how the woman could come up behind Jesus and wash his feet.

(Page 35) **washed my feet . . . greet me with a kiss . . . pour olive oil on my head:** Guests in a home were usually offered water so they could wash their feet, because most people either went barefoot or wore sandals and would come in the house with very dusty feet. Guests were also greeted with a kiss on the cheek, and special ones often had sweet-smelling olive oil poured on their head.

Page 35) **saved:** Or "healed." The Greek word may have either meaning.

Page 36) **hard:** Some manuscripts add "for people who trust in their wealth." Others add "for the rich."

Page 38) **in charge of collecting taxes:** See the note on page 20.

Page 38) **pay back four times as much:** Both Jewish and Roman law said that a person must pay back four times the amount that was taken.

Page 38) **saved:** Zacchaeus was Jewish, but it is only now that he is rescued from sin and placed under God's care.

Page 38) **son of Abraham:** As used in this verse, the words mean that Zacchaeus is truly one of God's special people.

Page 42) **temple helper:** A man from the tribe of Levi, whose job it was to work around the temple.

Page 43) **olive oil and wine:** In the New Testament times these were used as medicine. Sometimes olive oil is a symbol of healing by means of a miracle.

Page 45) **Tax collectors:** See the note on page 20.

Page 47) **pigs:** The Jewish religion taught that pigs were not fit to eat or even to touch. A Jewish man would have felt terribly insulted if he had to feed pigs, much less eat with them.

(Page 47) **what the pigs were eating:** The Greek text has "(bean) pods," which came from a tree in Palestine. These were used to feed animals. Poor people sometimes ate them too.

(Page 47) **ring . . . sandals:** These show that the young man's father fully accepted him as his son. A ring was a sign of high position in the family. Sandals showed that he was a son instead of a slave, since slaves did not usually wear sandals.

(Page 49) **our food for today:** Or "the food that we need" or "our food for the coming day."

(Page 49) **sins . . . others:** Or "what we owe . . . what others owe."

(Page 49) **evil:** Or "evil one," that is, the devil. Some manuscripts add, "The kingdom, the power, and the glory are yours forever. Amen."

(Page 50) **tax collectors:** See the note on page 20.

(Page 51) **don't let anyone know about it:** The Greek text has, "don't let your left hand know what your right hand is doing."

(Page 52) **live longer:** Or "grow taller."

(Page 52) **Solomon with all his wealth:** The Jewish people thought that Solomon was the richest person who had ever lived.

(Page 54) **leprosy:** See the note on page 26.

Page 54) **poured perfume on my body to prepare it for burial:** The Jewish people taught that giving someone a proper burial was even more important than helping the poor.

Page 55) **Iscariot:** This may mean "a man from Kerioth" (a place in Judea). But more probably it means "a man who was a liar" or "a man who was a betrayer."

Page 58) **the two brothers, James and John:** The Greek text has "the two sons of Zebedee."

Page 58) **having me drink from this cup:** In the Scriptures "to drink from a cup" sometimes means to suffer.

Page 58) **Are you still sleeping and resting?** Or "You may as well keep on sleeping and resting."

Page 60) **the man I greet with a kiss:** It was the custom for people to greet each other with a kiss on the cheek.

Page 60) **why are you here?:** Or "do what you came for."

Page 61) **some people who would tell lies about him in court:** The Law of Moses taught that witnesses were necessary before a person could be put to death.

Page 61) **Son of God:** One of the titles used for the kings of Israel.

Page 61) **right side:** The place of power and honor.

(Page 63) **a potter's field:** Perhaps a field owned by someone who made clay pots. But it may have been a field where potters came to get clay or to make pots or to throw away their broken pieces of pottery.

(Page 64) **Jesus Barabbas:** In this passage many manuscripts read "Barabbas."

(Page 65) **washed his hands:** To show that he was innocent.

(Page 66) **fortress:** The place where the Roman governor stayed. It was probably at Herod's palace west of Jerusalem, though it may have been Fortress Antonio north of the temple, where the Roman troops were stationed.

(Page 66) **scarlet robe:** This was probably a Roman soldier's robe.

(Page 66) **Place of the Skull:** The place was probably given this name because it was near a large rock in the shape of a human skull.

(Page 68) **Eli . . . sabachthani:** These words are in Aramaic, a language spoken in Palestine during the time of Jesus.

(Page 68) **Elijah:** In Aramaic the name "Elijah" sounds like "Eli," which means "my God."

(Page 68) **Elijah will come:** Many of the Jewish people expected the prophet Elijah to come and prepare the way for the Messiah.

(Page 68) **curtain in the temple:** There were two curtains in the temple. One was at the entrance, and the other separated the holy place from the most holy place that the Jewish people thought of as God's home on earth. The second curtain is probably the one that is meant.

(Page 68) **of James and John:** The Greek text has "of Zebedee's sons."

(Page 69) **tomb . . . solid rock:** Some of the Jewish people buried their dead in rooms carved into solid rock. A heavy stone was rolled against the entrance.

(Page 69) **the first one:** Probably the belief that Jesus is the Messiah.

(Page 71) **governor:** Pontius Pilate.

LIST OF PASSAGES

JESUS HELPS PEOPLE

JESUS TEACHES

THE END AND THE NEW BEGINNING

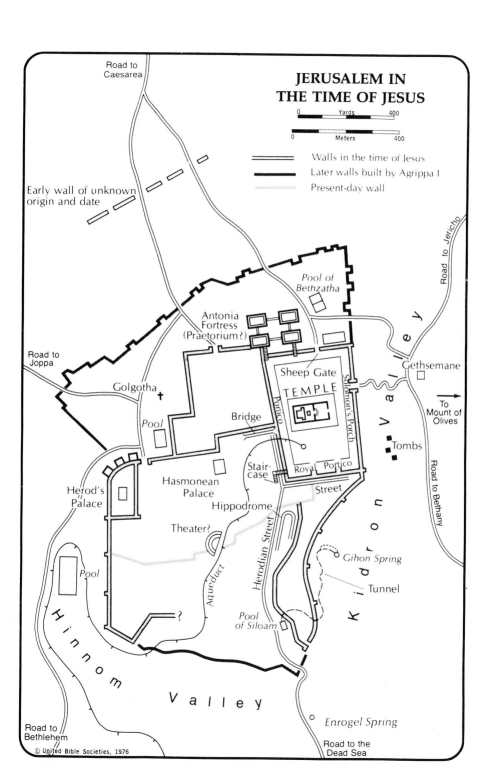

Road to
Caesarea

JERUSALEM IN
THE TIME OF JESUS

0   Yards   400

0   Meters   400

══════ Walls in the time of Jesus
━━━━━━ Later walls built by Agrippa I
········· Present-day wall

Early wall of unknown
origin and date

Pool of
Bethzatha

Antonia
Fortress
(Praetorium?)

Road to
Joppa

Sheep Gate

Road to Jericho

Gethsemane

Golgotha

TEMPLE

To
Mount of
Olives

Pool

Bridge

Portico

Solomon's Porch

Tombs

Staircase

Royal   Portico

Street

Road to Bethany

Herod's
Palace

Hasmonean
Palace

Hippodrome

Herodian Street

Theater?

Kidron Valley

Pool

Aqueduct

Gihon Spring

Tunnel

?

Pool
of Siloam

Hinnom

Valley

Enrogel Spring

Road to
Bethlehem

© United Bible Societies, 1976

Road to the
Dead Sea

PALESTINE IN THE TIME OF JESUS

0 Miles 40

0 Kms 40

Sidon

Abila
ABILENE

Damascus

Zarephath

LEBANON MTS.

SYRIA

MT. HERMON

Tyre

PHOENICIA

MEDITERRANEAN

Caesarea Philippi

SEA

GALILEE

Ptolemais

Chorazin

Bethsaida

Capernaum

Lake

Magadan

MT. CARMEL

Cana   Tiberias

Galilee

Nazareth

MT. TABOR

Nain

Gadara

Caesarea

DECAPOLIS

Salim

SAMARIA   Aenon

Samaria

Gerasa

MT. EBAL

MT. GERIZIM   Sychar

Jordan River

P
E
R
E
A

Joppa

Arimathea?

Ephraim

Jericho

Emmaus

Bethany

Azotus

Jerusalem

Qumran

Ascalon

JUDEA

Bethlehem

Gaza

Hebron

Dead

Sea

IDUMEA

N
A
B
A
T
E
A